BRITISH RAILWAY WAGONS 1980–2015

John Dedman

Front Cover: The evening Fort William to Mossend Speedlink at Rannoch on 1 July 1991. The locos are Nos 37406 and 37413, followed by six empty fuel oil tanks, four empty china clay tanks, two wagons loaded with rolls of paper and two wagons with aluminium ingots.

Rear Cover: Railfreight grey No. 26037 departing Mossend Yard on 12 July 1990 with one VEA van and six VGA vans.

First published 2016

Amberley Publishing
The Hill, Stroud
Gloucestershire, GL5 4EP

www.amberley-books.com

Copyright © John Dedman, 2016

The right of John Dedman to be identified as the Author of this work has been asserted in accordance with the Copyrights, Designs and Patents Act 1988.

ISBN 978 1 4456 6182 7 (print)
ISBN 978 1 4456 6183 4 (ebook)

All rights reserved. No part of this book may be reprinted or reproduced or utilised in any form or by any electronic, mechanical or other means, now known or hereafter invented, including photocopying and recording, or in any information storage or retrieval system, without the permission in writing from the Publishers.

British Library Cataloguing in Publication Data.
A catalogue record for this book is available from the British Library.

Typesetting by Amberley Publishing.
Printed in the UK.

BRITISH RAILWAY WAGONS
1980–2015

Introduction

It was my interest in model railways that led me to photograph more than just locomotives. Photographs of coaches and wagons that were of interest were also taken for reference for railway modelling. The wagon photographs in this book have been selected from my collection with a few additions from railway contacts. I have arranged the photographs roughly alphabetically to follow the TOPS code. As on the prototype, the brake vans are at the rear.

For the uninitiated reader I have included here a very basic explanation of the principles of the wagon TOPS codes used in this book.

The codes consist of three letters.
The first letter is the type of wagon group.
Examples are: O – Open, H – Hopper, M – Mineral, P – Privately Owned, S – Steel, T – Tank, V – Van, Y – Bogie Departmental wagons, Z – Four Wheel Departmental Wagon.
The second letter is the type, size or weight of wagon within its group.
The third letter is the type of brake used. A – Air Brake, B – Air Brake with through vacuum pipe, O – Unfitted, V – Vacuum Brake, W – Vacuum Brake with through air pipe.

Some common examples are:

CPV, which is a cement pressflo that is vacuum braked.
TTA, which is an air-braked 45-ton four-wheeled tank.
OBA is an air-braked open wagon.
VDA is an air-braked van.

Each photograph has a caption with information about the wagon; most include the wagon number, the TOPS wagon code, the wagon use and some will cover the services the wagon is used on and destination details. I have not included all the wagon building lot numbers and codes as these are all available in other publications.

The author and publisher would like to thank the following people for permission to use their photographs in this book: John Fox, Andy Picton, Pete Nurse and Steve Mosedale. They are credited on the respective captions and the inclusion of their images has given the book more variation of wagon types and filled some gaps in my own collection.

I would also like to acknowledge the help and information supplied by Andrew P. Wright, Mark Jamieson, David Hayes and David Ratcliffe.

A view of Mossend Yard on 10 July 1990 showing the variety of wagons that pass through this busy location. Nos 20185 and 20148 are ready to depart north with a Speedlink working.

BAA 900162 in Railfreight red livery at Toton on 10 June 1992. It is in the formation of the Lackenby–Corby steel coil train, which was referred to as the 'Tubeliner'. The red cradles are fitted for the carriage of steel coil.

Another wagon in the same train is BZA 900023, carrying four coils with the addition of the double arrows and Railfreight sign. Variations in end stantions can be seen on the neighbouring wagons. Toton 10 June 1992.

BBA 910486 is at Newport with steel coil loaded eye to the sky on 27 September 1990.

BBA 910218 with a steel slab load at Newport, 6 April 1998.

Built in the late 1950s, BVW B949060 is passing through Barnetby on 8 June 1992 with imported steel coil, travelling from Grimsby to Tinsley Yard at Sheffield. Two of the wagons in the formation have had the coil cradles painted Railfreight red, although most of the wagons are covered in rust.

A South Wales–Southampton Down Yard working is passing Eastleigh on 5 September 1984; the train is made up of TSV bitumen tanks for Fawley and steel coil wagons for Hamworthy. The steel wagons are a mixture of JGV bogie and SFV four-wheeled wagons for carrying steel coil, which is imported at Hamworthy. The SFV wagons were purpose built for steel coil, while the JGV bogie wagons are ex-Warflats that have had cradles fitted to hold the steel coils.

BNX B949517 is a bogie strip coil wagon passing through Salisbury on the Severn Tunnel–Eastleigh Speedlink on 9 April 1987.

SPA 460831 has a load of rod coil at Bevois Park Yard, Southampton. The red livery is very faded, especially when compared to the freshly painted neighbouring wagon. 25 September 1986.

A Sliding roof Tiphook wagon is passing through Toton Yard on 23 September 1993. These 90-ton wagons were used mainly for steel products, but were also used for other products.

Cargowaggon introduced their German-built 23-metre-long bogie bolster wagons in the late 1980s. Wagon number 30.80.4647.022-9 is in the Scunthorpe steelworks on 19 April 2014. It is loaded with sections of rail and could take a load of 64 tons.

Tiphook sliding hood wagons are used for carrying steel coil; this one is passing through Newport on a trip working from East Usk Yard to Alexandra Dock Junction Yard. When first introduced in the 1980s these wagons were in VTG grey and blue colours, but in 1994 were taken over by Tiphook and repainted into their blue livery. 6 April 1998.

The 6O32 10.00 Margam–Dollands Moor service carries steel to Europe via the Channel Tunnel. At Didcot, on 17 September 2015, the final wagon in the train is coil hood number 37 84 4667 045-7, which is registered by the Netherlands Railways. This is indicated by the 84 in the twelve digit number. This train is made up of a mixture of these wagons in blue livery and similar wagons in brown livery, which are registered by the French National Railways.

Still in its 1980s Railfreight red livery in 2015 is BDA 950223 with a steel load, seen in Didcot Yard on 17 September 2015. These wagons were originally bogie bolster D built in the 1950s, but were then upgraded in the 1970s with air brakes and Y25C bogies.

Iron Ore tippler wagons are used to carry imported iron ore from docks to steelworks. They are fitted with rotary couplings so that individual wagons can be rotated and unloaded without being uncoupled. JUA 26701 is in British Steel livery at Cardiff on 1 March 1995 and is in use between Port Talbot and Llanwern steelworks.

The end wagons of the iron ore tippler sets had conventional couplings on the outer end, as shown on JTA 26674 at Newport on 8 September 1993.

A pair of Tunnel Cement 22-ton CPV Pressflow hopper wagons at Bevois Park Yard in Southampton, 19 September 1986; they are B887956 and B887953. The Tunnel Cement name has all but disappeared on the side of the wagons. In 1985 there were three Tunnel Cement trains a week between Southampton Up Yard and Tring cutting, but only one working by 1986.

Blue Circle Cement CPV 8731 is at Westbury on 11 May 1985. The brackets can be seen on the body of the grey-liveried wagon where the company name board was once attached.

Pressflo CPV 888335 in bauxite livery, also at Westbury on 11 May 1985.

A Cement Pressflow at Eastleigh in the formation of the Speedlink to Severn Tunnel Junction on 8 March 1985. This Pressflo has a through air pipe and is coded CPW; it was originally built as a ferry wagon, as shown by the yellow hooks on the wagon side. Also in the formation is an empty HEA, an OBA loaded with timber, a VAA van and a Cartic Four loaded with Ford cars.

Blue Circle Presflo hopper PCA APCM 9106 was built in 1973 and is at Westbury station after arriving from the nearby cement works on 11 June 1987. These distinctively shaped wagons replaced the vacuum-braked Pressflos on block cement services.

PCA BCC10831 is on the Earles Sidings to Handsworth Cement at Toton, 1 October 1992.

In the mid-1980s, Blue Circle Cement introduced the Metalair bulk cement wagon. This one is PCA BCC 11123 on the rear of the Earles Sidings–Handsworth cement train, which also included the depressed centre wagons heading south past Toton Yard on 1 October 1992.

Blue Circle cement PCAs at Peak Forest. They are a mixture of dip tanks and Metalair straight body. The train loco is No. 45066 and is waiting to head south. 16 July 1986.

TCA TC9491 was one of four bulk cement wagons built for Tunnel Cement in 1977, seen here at Bevois Park Yard in Southampton on 25 September 1986. These wagons replaced the CPV Pressflos on Tunnel Cement trains between here and Tring Cutting.

Rugby Cement PCA PR 10000 is at Bevois Park Yard at Southampton. Rugby and Tunnel Cement companies both used the Up yard at Southampton. Blue Circle had their works in the Down yard at Northam, which is now the location of the South West Trains Traincare depot. 25 September 1986.

PCA RC10034 is in the attractive RMC orange livery at Didcot on 2 August 2010. These wagons are used to carry lime mortar from Peak Forest to Bletchley. This wagon was previously operated by Rugby Cement.

PCA VTG 74039 was built in France in 1985 and was originally in service with Rugby Cement between Halling and Southampton. On 18 June 2009 it is at Peak Forest in the Castle Cement livery.

Blue Circle used PDA bogie cement wagons between Southampton and Northfleet, often in the company of the four-wheel PCAs. They were built in 1969 and had a 79-ton capacity. PDA 9750 is on the rear of the train from Northfleet as it passes Eastleigh on 14 September 1985.

Two Croxton and Garry bogie twin dip tank wagons are behind loco No. 60061 with a southbound Enterprise service at Warrington on 13 August 1998. The clean example is CG 9743. They were used to carry calcium carbonate between Aberdeen and Sittingbourne in Kent. These wagons are now coded JCA but were previously PDA in cement service with Blue Circle.

The most common wagon used for transporting nuclear waste from power stations to Sellafield is the FNA flask wagon. The chassis is constructed of stainless steel and looks silver when clean, but generally ends up weathered brown. FNA 550044 and PFA DRSL 92730 are heading north along the Cumbrian coast at Parton behind No. 37603 on 14 September 2013.

No. 37688 *Kingmoor TMD* is heading north past the Seascale golf course on 14 July 2011 with two ex-works loaded PFAs from Drigg to Sellafield. The wagons are DRSL 92712 and DRSL 92731. These wagons were originally used by Cawoods for carrying coal containers. This is a trip working returning to Sellafield from Drigg, where low-level waste is disposed of.

The 6Z40 Crewe–Keyham is formed of No. 66421 and KUA MODA 95771. This wagon is used between the Naval Dockyard at Plymouth and Sellafield. Taunton 8 January 2013.

B999115 is an ex-BAA steel wagon now coded FDA. It is carrying a flask from Sellafield to Winfrith in Dorset and is hauled by a Class 73 with two RNA barrier wagons and a CAR brake at Salisbury on 2 May 1991.

Merry-go-round coal hoppers were designed to run between coal mines and power station. The wagons would be slowly drawn through the loader at the colliery, and discharged with automatic unloading equipment while on the move at the power station. HAA 365010 has its framework in Railfreight red livery at Toton on 1 October 1992.

From Railfreight sectorisation in 1987, some HAAs were repainted in the coal sector livery, which replaced the Railfreight red frames with yellow and the yellow and black diamond coal logo, as seen here on HAA 358427 at Toton. 1 October 1992.

Later in their lives many HAAs were fitted with canopies to stop coal dust blowing on to the lineside, which had caused complaints. HFA 358930 is an example at Toton on 23 September 1993. It has the coal sector logo on the side and is labelled Ayr, showing it was previously used in Scotland.

Domestic coal hopper HEA 361712, still in bauxite livery but very rusty, passing through Cardiff 8 September 1993.

HEA360552, also seen at Cardiff, is in the later Railfreight red and grey livery, complete with the Railfreight sign and double arrow logo. 26 May 1994.

No. 08845 is tripping two loaded Railfreight red HEAs from Bevois Park Yard to Dibbles Wharf at Southampton – each wagon has a different grade of coal load. 19 September 1986.

A few HEA wagons were brought back into use by DB Schenker in 2014 for use between Southampton and Mossend Yard in Glasgow. They are used to carry gravel from the Southampton Western Docks for B&Q on wagonload services via Eastleigh, Didcot and Warrington, usually two or three wagons at a time. EWS-liveried Nos 360485 and 360503 are in Didcot Yard after arrival from Eastleigh on 17 September 2015.

Lime-stained CBA 250004 is at Warrington on the 6V23 15.37 Hardendale Quarry–Margam limestone working. These wagons are very similar to the HAA but with an opening roof for loading and load protection. 7 June 1995.

The CDA china clay hoppers were introduced in 1987 and replaced the old wooden-bodied UCV wagons in Cornwall. As with the CBA they were similar to the HAA coal hoppers, with the addition of an opening roof. No. 375101 is in EWS livery at the tail end of the 11.27 Fowey–Goonbarrow empty china clay hoppers at Lostwithiel on 15 March 2012.

Cawoods Coal containers were used to export coal from Liverpool to Ireland. They were carried on PFA wagons; this one is No. 92726 at Warrington and is part of the 6V07 09.16 Seaforth Docks–Coedbach Washery train. On this day it was hauled by No. 37896. 19 August 1993.

MEA wagons were built in the early 1990s with new bodies on redundant HEA wagon chassis; most of them were originally used for carrying coal. EWS-liveried MEA 391335 is now in service at Peak Forest and carrying stone. 18 October 2015.

Mainline blue-liveried MEA 391123 is also at Peak Forest in aggregate service. The original livery for these wagons in Railfreight sectorisation era was grey with yellow ends. 18 June 2009.

Tiphook KFA 93262 is in Ministry of Defence service at Didcot, 9 July 1998. It is carrying the distinctive red MoD containers.

Warflat KFB MODA 96241 is carrying FU432 armoured personnel carriers at Eastleigh on 5 November 1992. These wagons are fitted with jacks located under the buffers, which are screwed down for loading and unloading. This example was built in 1976 and is air-braked with a through vacuum pipe.

On 15 February 2010 the 6X38 Marchwood–Didcot service carried a selection of military vehicles on Warflat and Warwell wagons. Included was warflat KFA 95234 with two Saxon armoured personnel carriers, seen here coming off the Fawley branch at Totton.

In the same formation is KFA MODA 95254 carrying a Sparton armoured personnel carrier and a FV105 Sultan Command and Control vehicle. This wagon is also from the same batch as the previous two photographs. 15 February 2010.

Warwell KWB 95508 is from a batch that was built during the Second World War. In the 1970s it was fitted with Gloucester GPS bogies and air brakes. It is carrying a red Warrior infantry section vehicle at Totton on 20 January 2010 as part of the 7X38 Marchwood–Didcot.

Warwell KWB 95508 is again at Totton on 14 April 2010, this time carrying a FV105 Sultan Command and Control vehicle. It is the final wagon on the 6X36 Marchwood–Didcot service.

BRT 7781 was originally one of the blue covered grain hoppers, which were built in the 1960s. In the 1980s some of them were fitted with new suspension and air brakes for use in the Speedlink network. No. 7781 is on display at the Andover Rail event on 22 March 1986.

Grainflow Polybulk PIA 33 70 9280 075 was built in 1984; it is in the process of being re-marshalled in Mossend Yard on 10 July 1990.

In its striking blue-and-white striped livery, Distillers Polybulk 33 70 9280 009 is in the yard at Mossend on 10 July 1990.

Ex-grain wagon Distillers Polybulk 33 70 9280 002 is in limestone service in the Hardendale–Margam train at Warrington on 10 August 1998.

STS polybulk PIA 33 70 9382 122 in its striking orange livery departing from the Up yard at Southampton. 28 February 1985.

Polybulk wagon number 33RIV 70BR 938 2010-4 is in Traffic Services Ltd livery at Didcot on 2 August 1994. It is in china clay service and returning to Cornwall from the continent; this service normally ran about once every two weeks.

A covered bogie hopper in the number series 33 87 5699 is passing through Cardiff. It is in service carrying silicate sand from France to Dow Corning at Barry Docks on 1 March 1995.

NACCO Bogie Covhop 33 70 0834 128-4 is loaded with potash from Boulby mine and is taking the Tees Dock branch at Grangetown on 22 October 2015.

Built in France in the late 1980s, Cerestar powder hopper 33 70 9292-204 is bringing up the rear of a southbound Enterprise working from Mossend as it arrives at Warrington Bank Quay on 10 August 1998.

Cerestar powder hoppers were used for transporting starch from Manchester to paper mills in Scotland for corn products. After re-marshalling, PBA 11300 is part of a Speedlink trip working heading north from Mossend Yard to Thornton Junction and eventually Aberdeen. 10 July 1990.

PCA PR10014 is in the same service as the bogie hoppers in the previous photos, seen here passing north through Warrington on a Mossend-bound Enterprise service on 7 June 1995.

Yeoman aggregate hopper PGA PR14084 is at Westbury 23 May 1991. These 38-ton air-braked hopper wagons replaced 21-ton vacuum-braked hopper wagons on services from Foster Yeoman's quarry at Merehead in Somerset to various destinations around London and the south east.

Aggregate hopper wagon PGA PR14117 is very similar to the Yeoman PGA but is in the ARC mustard livery at Westbury on 11 June 1987. ARC operated from the Whately quarry with similar destinations as Yeoman in the south east.

A Procor PGA in E.C.C. Quarries Croft Granite livery; part of the number is obscured by rust but it appears to be in the number series 143xx. It is seen arriving at Westbury on 11 June 1987.

Tiger Rail POA TRL5387 at Salisbury on 12 October 1989. This wagon is in service with Yeoman and returning to Meldon Quarry on a train from Botley in Hampshire.

Procor PTA PR 26826 was built in 1972 and was originally used for iron ore service on Teeside until made redundant by steelworks closure. It was taken over by Procor and is now hired to ARC for aggregate service. Now in the ARC mustard livery it is in the formation of the 6O89 16.05 Westbury–Eastleigh at the end of its journey on 29 March 1985.

Foster Yeoman PHA PR17831 is from a batch of Procor bogie hoppers introduced in 1984 for use from Merehead quarry to Theale in Berkshire. Andover, 22 March 1986.

PHA OK 19372 was one of a batch of 100 bogie hoppers built by Orenstein & Koppel in 1989. It is in use by Foster Yeoman between Merehead Quarry and various destinations and is at Westbury on 23 May 1991.

PGA PR 8260 is at Warrington on 19 August 1993 – the wagon is operated by CAIB for transporting salt from Runcorn. The wagons are sheeted to keep the load dry and prevent rust spreading.

PGA PR8280 Warrington, 10 August 1998.

Dutch-liveried No. 31154 has just departed Latchford Sidings at Warrington with six PGA salt hoppers covered with CAIB tarpaulins. 10 August 1998.

PNA GWS 5267 was originally B715029, a BR ferry fitted open wagon coded OJA. It was acquired in 1988 by the Great Western Society Railway Centre at Didcot and was used for delivering coal to the centre from Didcot West Yard. It and sister wagon PNA GWS 5268, ex-B715029, were both withdrawn during October 2015. Captured here on 11 June 1998.

Another wagon from Great Western Society is PFW GWS 91200, a modified GWR 1939-built chaired sleeper wagon that had planked sides added. These wagons were previously used for carrying concrete products for the railway and some were labelled Taunton Concrete. It is parked outside the GWS centre on 11 June 1998 and is loaded with steam locomotive wheels and a small container.

Pipe wagon B741574 has been preserved in bauxite livery and is at Buckfastleigh on the Dart Valley Railway. These wagons were built by BR in the 1950s to a similar LNER design. This particular wagon has air pipes. 13 March 2012.

The ODA is an ex-pipe wagon that has been fitted with air brakes, new suspension and roller bearings. They were used by the MoD in Speedlink services, their short wheelbase making them more suitable for the tight curves in some of their bases than the newer long-wheelbase OAA and OBA wagons. Railfreight red-and grey-liveried No. 113036 is at Southampton Up yard on the rear of the evening Speedlink to Eastleigh, 29 March 1985.

ODA 113041 and OAA 100054 are in the formation of the Marchwood–Salisbury Speedlink working on 10 April 1986. The ODA is in the Railfreight red and grey livery and the OAA in the original maroon livery with the double arrow logo unusually in reverse.

OCA 112262 is at Didcot on the rear of the arriving Enterprise train from Eastleigh. The OCAs were used for carrying general merchandise and steel products. 29 July 1996.

On 22 March 1986 there was a rail event at Andover with a small selection of modern wagons and locos on display – included was OBA 110678 in its red and grey Railfreight livery. The OBA was a 31-ton general purpose open wagon. Many were later transferred to the civil engineers' fleet and recoded ZDA with the name 'Bass'.

This scene at Carrbridge in Scotland shows OBAs in timber traffic. No. 37262 *Dounreay* has arrived from the north with loaded wagons and will return north with the empty wagons in the foreground. OBA 110573 is the wagon nearest to the camera on 29 May 1989.

OTA timber wagons were built from OCA and VDA wagons; No. 112225 was in a batch converted from OCA open wagons with extended square ends. Cardiff, 8 September 1993.

OTA 112167 was also built from an OCA wagon but has the higher angled ends. Both of these OTAs were on a trainload of timber through Cardiff on 8 September 1993.

MDW B310440 is vacuum braked but with a through air pipe and is being used to carry scrap metal. It is part of an unfitted freight train at South Bank on Teeside, 4 July 1988.

PRA RLS 6308 was one of a batch of open wagons built in 1983. As they were used for china clay traffic, they had tarpaulin covers to protect the load. They travelled on Speedlink services between Cornwall and Fort William. Five of these wagons were on the Up evening Speedlink at Dawlish Warren on 9 April 1985.

Storage Transport Systems TTA 53116 is in china clay service, indicated by the spillage on the tank side. It is in the formation of the Eastleigh–Quidhampton Speedlink trip working at Salisbury on 12 October 1989. (John Fox)

Ferry-fitted bogie English China Clays Ltd tank is in the process of being remarshalled in the yard at Bescot on 16 July 1992. The code is TIA and the wagon is numbered 83 70 7895 203. Five of these tanks came from France in 1987 and were used to replace the TTA tanks in the previous photo.

Two Tiger TEA bogie tanks are part of a Quidhampton–Eastleigh trip working at Salisbury on 12 October 1989. They are in service with English China Clay and will be remarshalled at Eastleigh before heading to Scotland.

New bogie tanks were built in France in 1989 for the movement of china clay slurry for ECC from Burngullow in Cornwall to Irvine in Scotland. When new these wagons got the nickname of silver bullets due to their shiny stainless steel finish. Wagon number 33 70 7890 116-8 is on the southbound working from Irvine, which had paused at Warrington Bank Quay on 7 June 1995.

VTG Bogie TIA ferry tank number 33 70 7895 161-9 was built in the mid-1980s and is operated by English China Clays. It is being remarshalled at Salisbury after loading at Quidhampton; it will be joined by MoD wagons from Dinton and then tripped to Eastleigh. It will then head for Scotland via the Speedlink network. (John Fox)

TCA 78802 is one of five bogie tanks in the number series 78800 to 78804, originally built in 1975 for acid service. In 1981 they were modified to carry china clay slurry, painted in the blue ECC livery and were used on services from Cornwall and Quidhampton to Warrington, Mossend and Aberdeen. Two of these bogie tanks are on the rear of the 6M69 13.57 Cardiff Canton–Warrington Enterprise at Newport on 6 April 1998.

Six-wheeled ex-milk tank number 041340 is at Tinsley Depot on 22 September 1984. The large label on the right-hand end reads 'Anti-Freeze Storage Only' and underneath is an original label – 'Unigate Creameries Ltd E834'. On the left-hand end the sign reads, 'Not To Be Used For Milk'.

I.C.I. Chlor-Chemicals TTA ICIM 70809 was one of a batch of twenty wagons built in 1977 for I.C.I. Mond in the number sequence 70800 to 70819. These tanks carry caustic soda from Runcorn to Scotland and have arrived at Warrington from the north. 7 June 1995.

TTA STL 51952 is one of a batch of six acid tanks built in 1983. The Hazchem 2P1830 refers to the Sulphuric Acid cargo, some of which has burnt away parts of the warning signs. Warrington, 7 June 1995.

Procor tank TTA PR58528 is on the rear of a Speedlink departing north at 09.10 from Mossend Yard on 10 July 1990. It was originally used for caustic soda but is seen here carrying molasses destined for Menstrie.

No. 47365 *Diamond Jubilee* is departing south from Warrington with a mixed freight. The first wagon is Associated Octel tank TIB 23 70 739 0 411 0, which is ferry fitted. It is one of a batch of seven wagons built in 1965 and is used to carry lead anti-knock compound, the Hazchem reads 2WE 1649. The yellow sign on the side of the tank lists emergency procedures and the green dome on the top is a protective cover for the loading and unloading valves and connections. 18 August 1993.

LPG was shipped from Furzebrook at the BP Wytch Farm oil field in Dorset to BP LPG Terminal at Hallen Marsh at Avonmouth. TTA BPO 59786 is part of the 6V13 13.20 from Furzebrook at Eastleigh in 1998. The LPG trains from Furzebrook to Avonmouth ran from 20 November 1990 until 22 July 2005. This tank still carries the Railfright Petroleum sub-sector blue and yellow logo from the late 1980s. (Steve Mosedale)

LPG tanks are pressurized and, to indicate this, they have white tanks with the orange waist band. The BP tanks are distinctive with their yellow solebars, as can be seen on TTA BPO 59573 at Eastleigh in 1998. They have no ladders or roof walkways, as the loading and unloading is carried out via the sliding door on the tank side. (Photo by Steve Mosedale)

Esso TTA 56095 is in Eastleigh Works on 12 October 1986; the oval on the side of the tank shows where the Esso logo was once carried. These 45-ton tanks were vacuum braked when first built in 1965 and later converted to air brakes.

Esso TTA 56121 has arrived at Westbury on 5 April 1990 in the formation of the 6V62 10.44 from Fawley to Tavistock Junction. This service ceased to run in October 2013.

Ex-works TTA ESSO 56036 is at Eastleigh on 11 September 2012. These wagons spent many years supplying diesel fuel from the Esso Fawley Refinery to British Rail depots and later some of the privatised rail companies depots. Loaded wagons were tripped from Fawley to Eastleigh, where they were re-marshalled into Speedlink and later Wagonload services to various destinations. The last of these wagons ran from Fawley in March 2015.

Shell Oil 45-ton TTA SUKO 67146 was built in 1967; it has a grey barrel, red solebar and black underframe, which was the standard livery for Class A tanks in the 1970s and 1980s. The tank is passing Warrington on 18 August 1993 in the formation of the 6M54 Leeds–Stanlow Railfreight Petroleum service.

TTA SUKO 67313 is in the later Shell Oil livery, with the red and yellow zigzag stripes, and the Railfreight Petroleum logo. It is part of a set of four tanks at Toton being tripped from the yard to the diesel depot. 10 October 1991.

TTA SUKO 67910 is at the loco refuelling point at Buxton Depot on 3 June 1993.

TTA BPO 67487 is at Southampton Up yard on 29 March 1985.

The loco refuelling point at Ipswich is supplied with fuel by rail. TTAs BPO 53773 and BPO 37263 are in use there on 16 July 1998.

A view of the ladder end of BPO 37263 being taken away by No. 08745. The tank is in the latest BP livery of green, which was introduced to their fleet of Class A tanks in 1990. This tank also has the blue and yellow Petroleum sub sector logo on the tank side. Ipswich, 16 July 1998.

Bitumen tank ESSO 44494 was the last one built in the 1963 batch of 44425 to 44494. They were originally coded TSV and vacuum braked, but were converted to air brakes during the 1980s and recoded TSA – the TOPS code being painted on in large white letters rather than the conventional TOPS panel. This wagon is in the 6B72 13.35 Fawley–Eastleigh service, approaching Southampton on 8 April 1988.

59

TTA 61745 was built in the late 1960s, originally as a BP tank. By the early 1990s it was operating from the Fawley Refinery for Esso and was eventually transferred to their fleet along with other similar BP bitumen tanks, which replaced the smaller barrelled tanks in the previous photo. Didcot, 2 August 1994.

TTA Esso 61949 was originally a Shell bitumen tank before transferring to the Esso fleet in the early 1990s. Seen here at Eastleigh bringing up the rear of a Fawley–Eastleigh working on 29 April 1993.

Caib TTA 49380 is an acetic acid tank indicated by the Hazchem code of 2P 2789. This cladded tank was built in 1975, originally as a TTB, but the vacuum through pipe has since been removed. It is in the 6V14 07:30 Hull–Baglan Bay at Newport on 6 April 1998.

British Oxygen Company had a fleet of forty 102-ton cryogenic bogie tanks numbered 84601 to 84640. TEA 84632 is at Warrington on 14 June 1990 in a train that is departing from Latchford sidings.

TDA 78005 was one of the Esso fleet of bogie LPG tanks used to carry propane or butane. One of their long standing flows was from Fawley Refinery to Longport, supplying the potteries with LPG. The white body with the orange stripe denotes a pressurised tank. Didcot, 29 July 1996.

A close-up view of the business end of LPG bogie tank TDA Esso 78011 at Didcot on 29 July 1996. It shows the bogie, the TOPS panel, the Hazchem label and the sliding door that covers the loading and unloading connections.

Liquid anhydrous ammonia tank number 33 70 7895 022 was built in 1980 and is fitted with a sun screen. It is owned by VTG and operated by I.C.I and is at Stenson Junction in the formation of the 6E55 11.10 Bromsgrove Unitank–Port Clarence. 7 September 1987.

In the same train as the previous photograph is a much cleaner VTG tank number 33 70 7892 046; the Hazchem code is 2PE1005. Ammonia is a highly toxic gas and classed as a dangerous cargo, which requires a barrier wagon at each end of the formation with a brake van on the rear. 7 September 1987.

TCA 78609 is another liquid anhydrous ammonia tank in the same train as the previous two photographs. This wagon was built in 1971 but is not ferry fitted like the wagons either side of it. 7 September 1987.

This pale blue TEA 100-ton bogie tank is used for carrying styrene monomer between Immingham Docks and Stalybridge. It was originally a Chevron Oil Class B tank and in 1990 it was converted for carrying styrene monomer along with four others in the number range PR82602 to 82606. On 14 August 1996 it is passing Stafford in the Washwood Heath-Longport Connectrail service and heading for Marcrofts at Stoke.

Tiphook bogie tank number 33 70 7899 025 was built in France in 1987. The tank is insulated and clad with stainless steel. The Hazchem indicates it is carrying caustic soda. Warrington, 19 August 1993.

TEA RLS 82214 is a lagged bogie tank in Class B service passing through Doncaster, 19 August 1993. (Steve Mosedale)

TEA BPO 87779 is in the latest BP green livery. It is in the formation of the 6V62 from Fawley to Tavistock Junction as it approaches Eastleigh. The 100-ton tanks will be detached in the yard and will go to Holybourne for another load of crude oil. 29 April 1993.

Arriving at Eastleigh from Fawley on 7 July 1998, in the same crude oil service, is TEA BPO 87469 in the earlier BP grey livery.

The wagons of the 6B43 11.50 Eastleigh–Fawley, including bitumen TSAs, gas oil TTAs and a tiger liquid chlorine tank between two ex-ferry vans in use as barrier wagons. The chlorine tank came from Sandbach and was used in the refinery in the manufacture of chlorobutyl rubber and lubricating additives.

VTG 23 80 7391 045 is a 40-ton ferry tank passing Warrington in the 6S61 Railfreight Distribution service from Arpley Yard to Dalry Roche. This tank is carrying glycol from Germany and would be detached at Carlisle and added to a service for its final destination of Middlesbrough.

67

Air-braked 45-ton van VAA 200056 was one of the first batch built in the late 1960s; here it is in Railfreight red and grey livery, which has replaced the earlier bauxite livery. This van is in MoD service and is part of an Eastleigh–Salisbury Speedlink working. 9 April 1987. (John Fox)

The Railfreight sectorisation Speedlink livery of grey with yellow ends has been applied to VAA 200118. The van has a ventilator fitted on the end and the Railfreight Speedlink logo with the red and yellow diamonds on the side. Cardiff, 27 September 1990.

VDA 201025 looks abandoned in a siding at Rannoch station on 30 June 1991. It is one of a batch built in the mid-1970s with FAT 13 suspension. As this van has a white roof, it was probably one of the fleet used by Rowntrees for the carrying of chocolate products.

VDA 201044 is another van with the FAT 13 suspension. It is in MoD service in a Speedlink working from Eastleigh at Salisbury, from where it will travel on to Dinton. 9 April 1987.

ZRA ADC 200654 is a former VDA van now in departmental service, seen here in a Speedlink working departing Mossend Yard on 27 June 1989.

VGA vans were introduced in the early 1980s, the sides consisting of two large sliding aluminium doors. No. 210511 is at Bevois Park Yard, Southampton, on 25 September 1986. It is in the original livery for these vans with Railfreight red ends and decorated with the double arrow logo and Railfreight and Speedlink signs on boards fitted to the doors.

VGA 210429 is in MoD service at Didcot on 11 June 1998. It is in the later Railfreight Distribution sectorisation livery with yellow ends. The sides are littered with used warning and hazard signs from previous trips.

A very clean Railfreight-liveried VEA van 230079 is at Salisbury on 19 October 1989; it is in the Speedlink from Eastleigh and will be tripped to Dinton MoD. (John Fox)

VEA Railfreight van 230521 is at Westbury on 1 November 1984. These vans had a wheelbase of 10 feet and were well suited for MoD sites where there were plenty of sharp curves. They were built in the 1960s and later modified in the early 1980s with air brakes and roller bearings for the Speedlink network.

The 6M93 14.28 Southampton Up Yard–Willesden Speedlink was made up of a good variety of wagons on 28 February 1985; VEA 230025 is followed by a bogie Cargowaggon ferry van.

On 16 August 1985 the Eastleigh–Severn Tunnel Junction Speedlink has four UKF PWA Palvans in its formation. These vans are used to carry fertiliser, which can be loaded with fork lift trucks via the large body-side doors.

German Cargowaggon 279 7 526-1 is in brown, as opposed to the usual blue livery for these vehicles. The side of the van is made up of three sliding doors, giving easy access for loading and unloading with fork lift trucks. Toton, 23 September 1993.

Tiphook ferry van 2693 030 is the final wagon of continental van train hauled by No. 47207, heading south past Toton Yard on 23 September 1993. These vans were built in Germany in 1985; they were 73 feet long, could carry 73 tons and had two large sliding doors.

The Whale bogie ballast wagon was a 50-ton development of the Southern Railway and Southern Region 40-ton Walrus wagon. DB982427 is air-braked, in grey and yellow livery and has three control wheels for the ballast chutes so ballast can be dropped in the centre or either side of the track. It is passing Coalville in the formation of the 7G01 Bardon Hill–Bescot service on 11 June 1986.

The Seacow is a 40-ton bogie ballast wagon fitted with air brakes and a through vacuum pipe, which gives it a TOPS code of YGB. DB980167 is in the engineers' Dutch livery of grey with a yellow band along the top of the wagon side and is fitted with Y27CS bogies. It is at Southampton on the rear of the 7V84 06.15 Three Bridges–Meldon Quarry on 8 April 1988.

The Mullet is used for carrying sections of rail. Yellow-liveried YLA DC 967578 is at Eastleigh on 2 June 2009.

Ventilated pallet vans were built from 1955 to 1961, when most of them were withdrawn. Some were retained and refurbished with new suspension and air brakes. ADB 781864 was one of those converted and is now in use by the mechanical engineers. It is in olive-green livery with the TOPS code ZRB and is arriving at Eastleigh from Hamworthy on 19 June 1985.

An unidentified Lowmac wagon at Tinsley diesel depot on 27 October 1995. It is labelled Lowmac EP and was built in 1950 to a LNER design. It has screw couplings and vacuum brakes but looks as if the brake hose has been removed from the buffer beam. By this date the only examples left in use were in departmental service and this one is probably an internal user for the depot. It is carrying the roof section from a Class 47 loco, which is probably being overhauled inside the maintenance building.

ZCA DB 982197 appears to be an ex-LMS three-plank wagon now in departmental use. It still has the remains of its bauxite livery but has the addition of air brakes – a useful wagon for the engineers with drop sides and drop ends, as can be seen in the photograph. Behind that are two ex-pipe wagons DB741211 and DB741570 in the attractive S&T blue livery. Warrington, 25 February 1993.

ZBV DB991617 is a 'Grampus' wagon built in 1959 and equipped with vacuum brakes. It has drop-down side doors and removable ends and was used for carrying ballast and sleepers. This one is in at Newport on 8 August 1996 and is in a typical rusty condition.

The Tope wagons were a conversion from the HTV 21-ton coal hopper wagons in the mid-1980s. The original body height was reduced and plates were fitted at the end of the hopper. They were vacuum braked and painted in the departmental grey livery with the yellow band. ZCV DB970178 is at Wigan on 6 June 1995.

In 1993 Gunnel wagons were converted from stone PGA wagons, which had their bodysides cut down and the ends extended. ZFA DC390651 is in the yard at Didcot on 11 June 1998.

KDB 730046 is an ex-tube wagon now in use with Satlink in the attractive red and yellow livery. The TOPS code of ZDW show it is vacuum braked with through air pipes. Toton Yard, 1 October 1992.

ZGV KDB 730837 is at Peak Forest on 3 June 1993; this is another ex-tube wagon in engineers service. The wagon has corrugated ends and the TOPS code is ZGV, indicating it is vacuum braked. It is loaded with concrete cable ducting sections. The similar wagon to the right is numbered KDB731741 and the different colours on the sides of both wagons show where planks of wood have been replaced.

Bringing up the rear of a rake of Rudd wagons loaded with dirty ballast is ZBA DB972090, heading north through Warrington on 7 June 1995. Rudds were built with new bodies fitted to the redundant chassis of 21-ton coal hoppers but fitted with air brakes.

ZDA DC 100037 is an ex-OAA wagon, which was among the first revenue air-braked open wagons built in the early 1970s. This example is in the civil engineer's livery of grey and yellow and carries the name *Squid*. The ends are metal and the wooden planked sides are made up of three drop-down doors. Eastleigh, 28 May 1992.

Two different styles of Engineers ZDA Bass wagons in the Dutch grey and yellow livery at Toton on 1 October 1992. The one on the left is an ex-OCA wagon, while the one on the right is an ex-OBA wagon, now numbered DC110068, and is also labelled Civil Link.

ZCA M110385 is a Sea Urchin in Mainline blue livery; it is passing Millbrook Freightliner Terminal in the formation of the Westbury–Eastleigh departmental working on 19 September 2007.

OBA 110451 has had its wooden drop-down sides replaced with wire mesh, and is seen here in EWS maroon livery with the ends still in the engineers' grey and yellow. It is in the Westbury–Eastleigh departmental working arriving at its destination on 4 September 2013. (Andy Picton)

A general view of part of the yard at Warrington on 25 February 1993. In the foreground are three ZDW ex-Pipe wagons in S&T blue livery; the right-hand one is DB 741948. Beyond them are two ballast wagons, a Dogfish and a Mermaid, then a blue-liveried GUV that has had a replacement door from a Royal Mail red-liveried example. Passing on the main line in the distance is No. 47241 with a train of liquid chlorine tanks, complete with a barrier wagon and a brake van on each end.

ZKV were ex-aggregate wagons, which were replaced by air-braked wagons. Still in its rust livery, DB388406 has been transferred to the engineers' department but not yet repainted. These wagons were originally built for iron ore service. Westbury, 5 April 1990.

DB388990 is another ZKV, but repainted into the Dutch livery of grey and yellow. The TOPS panel shows that, fully laden, it is rated at 26.5 tons. Westbury, 5 April 1990.

ZEV DB983749 was built in the early 1960s and was one of the final batch of Catfish 19-ton ballast hoppers. It was built with roller bearings and has the single control wheel for opening central chute doors to release the ballast between the rails. This one is in the engineers' Dutch livery of grey and yellow at Bescot on 18 August 1993.

ZCV Puffin DB983572 has been modified from a ZEV Catfish ballast wagon. The large wheel for controlling the ballast door has been removed from the other end of the wagon. It is at Bescot on 8 June 1995 and looks as if it is being used for bagged rubbish.

The Dogfish was a larger version of the Catfish. It had three control wheels for releasing the ballast centrally or either side of the rails via the chutes, which can be seen on the lower sides. ZFV DB993590 was built in 1960 and is at Toton on 23 September 1993 in the grey and yellow livery.

ZFV DB992860 is from an earlier build of Dogfish wagons from the late 1950s. The three handwheels can be seen for controlling the ballast chutes. Before the rust took over, the livery was probably departmental olive green or black. Toton, 23 September 1993.

Dogfish ZFV DB993586 was built in 1960 and is still in service at Didcot on 27 September 1996. It is in the hardly discernible olive-green livery and is fitted with roller bearings and vacuum brakes. On the solebar is the name Mainline, showing which of the three Railfreight sectors it belongs to in the run up to privatisation.

The Mermaid wagon has a body that can tip its ballast load either side of the track. ZJV DB989487 is at Cliffe Hill on 11 June 1986 and when loaded will depart as the 8E86 to Doncaster.

ZUB DB993924 is a 20-ton Shark van, one of the final batch to be built in 1962. It is on the rear of a southbound ballast train at Warrington in well-weathered olive-green livery, with the Transrail T marking on the side, and is air braked with a through vacuum pipe. 7 June 1995.

Shark van ZUV DB993829 was built in 1957 and looks like it has had a recent repaint into a bauxite livery. It is vacuum-braked with a high-level vacuum pipe. It is seen departing Didcot Yard behind No. 37709 on 9 July 1998. (Steve Mosedale)

Shark ZUV DB993835 has arrived at Didcot from the west at the head of a ballast train hauled by Mainline-liveried No. 37798 on 29 July 1996. This is another 1957-built van with the high-level vacuum pipes and is in the Dutch engineers' grey and yellow livery with the branding of its new owners Mainline Freight.

No. 08940 and CAP brake van B955055 are at Alexandra Dock Junction at Newport in 1985. (Pete Nurse)

Brake van B954734 is designated as CAR as it is air and vacuum piped, also indicated by the yellow panels on the sides and ends. The three small pipes on the bodyside connect the air brake pipe to the guard's gauge and valve inside the cabin. It is seen here at Southampton on the rear of the 6B72 13.35 Fawley–Eastleigh tanks on 11 April 1988. It is used on this trip as the train includes a liquid chlorine tank, classed as a dangerous product and requiring a brake van.

Withdrawn CAR brake van B955407 is at Warrington with other out of use vans on 18 August 1993. The van has roller bearings and the yellow panels have been labelled 'Air Piped'.

Bauxite-liveried B955136 is one of two CAR brake vans on an MGR coal train at Willington Power Station on 30 April 1987.

At the other end of the same train is Railfreight red-and grey-liveried B954779. These were required when the guard had to close crossing gates on colliery branch lines.

Railfreight-liveried CAR brake van B955160 is at Frodingham diesel depot on 8 June 1992. The warning on the side of the van is 'Caution! Narrow Step Boards'; these are painted white.

Brake van CAR B955213 is in Railfreight red and grey livery and is on the rear of the 7Z00 11.00 Winfrith–Gloucester flask at Beaulieu Road in the New Forest on 23 September 1986. The barrier wagon is an ex-British Rail ferry van, number B787199.

Brake van ZTR 955049 is in Railfreight red and grey livery with wasp stripes on the ends and is used for propelling moves. Sunderland, 1 October 1988.

CAR B954989 in Railfreight Distribution livery, but now out of use, is probably on its final journey in a Civil Link working at Warrington on 18 August 1993.

CAR B955062 is in Railfreight coal sector livery of grey and yellow with the sector logo on the side. This brake van was one of the final batch built in 1961 at Ashford. The guard is enjoying the sunshine on his veranda on the rear of the 7Z00 10.33 Winfrith–Gloucester nuclear flask working as it passes Eastleigh on 9 April 1992.

CAR B954781 was built in 1959 and had the through air pipe fitted in 1967. The end has been plated over and it has recently been painted in executive grey Railfreight livery with the coal sector logo on the side. Salisbury, 23 May 1991.

RAQ B955616 is in an off-white livery with Petroleum sub sector logos at Warrington on 10 August 1998.

Ex-Southern Railway Queen Mary bogie brake van ADS56296 is at Andover on 22 March 1986. It is in bauxite livery with wasp stripes on the ends and a TOPS code of YTX, showing it is dual braked. This van still has the sand boxes on the veranda ends and coach bogies, which give it a more comfortable ride than a four-wheel brake van.

Queen Mary KDS 56305 is in Signal and Telegraph livery and is coded YTW, vacuum braked and air piped. Twenty-five of these bogie brake vans were built by the Southern Railway in 1936 for express goods work. This one has been plated on the bodyside to the left of the guards ducket. It is on the rear of the southbound Carnforth to Arpley ballast train at Warrington on 13 August 1996.

ZTP 950213 is an ex-LMS brake van built in 1950; it is in the Signal and Telegraph red and yellow livery. It has a through vacuum pipe that was added later in its life. The photograph is misleading as the van is not on the rear of an MGR train – the HAA wagon and brake van are on the rear of the breakdown train as it arrives in Toton Yard on 10 October 1991. (John Fox)

Bibliography

Magazines

Rail Magazine
Rail Express Magazine
Freightmaster, various editions (Mark Rawlinson, issued four times a year)

Books

Gamble, G., *British Railway Wagons Engineer's Stock Volume 1* (1998)
Gamble, G., *British Railway Private Owner Wagons Volume 2* (2000)
Larkin, David, *Working Wagons Vol 4 1985–1992* (2002)
Larkin, David, *Wagons of the Middle British Railways Era* (2007)
Marsden, Colin J., *Rolling Stock Recognition 2: BR and Private Owner Wagons* (1984)
Ratcliffe, David, *Modern Private Owner Wagons on British Rail* (1989)
Ratcliffe, David, *International Train-Ferry Wagons in Colour* (2009)
Smith, Tom, *British Railway Air-Braked Stock Volume 1* (2002)